W9-AVK-448

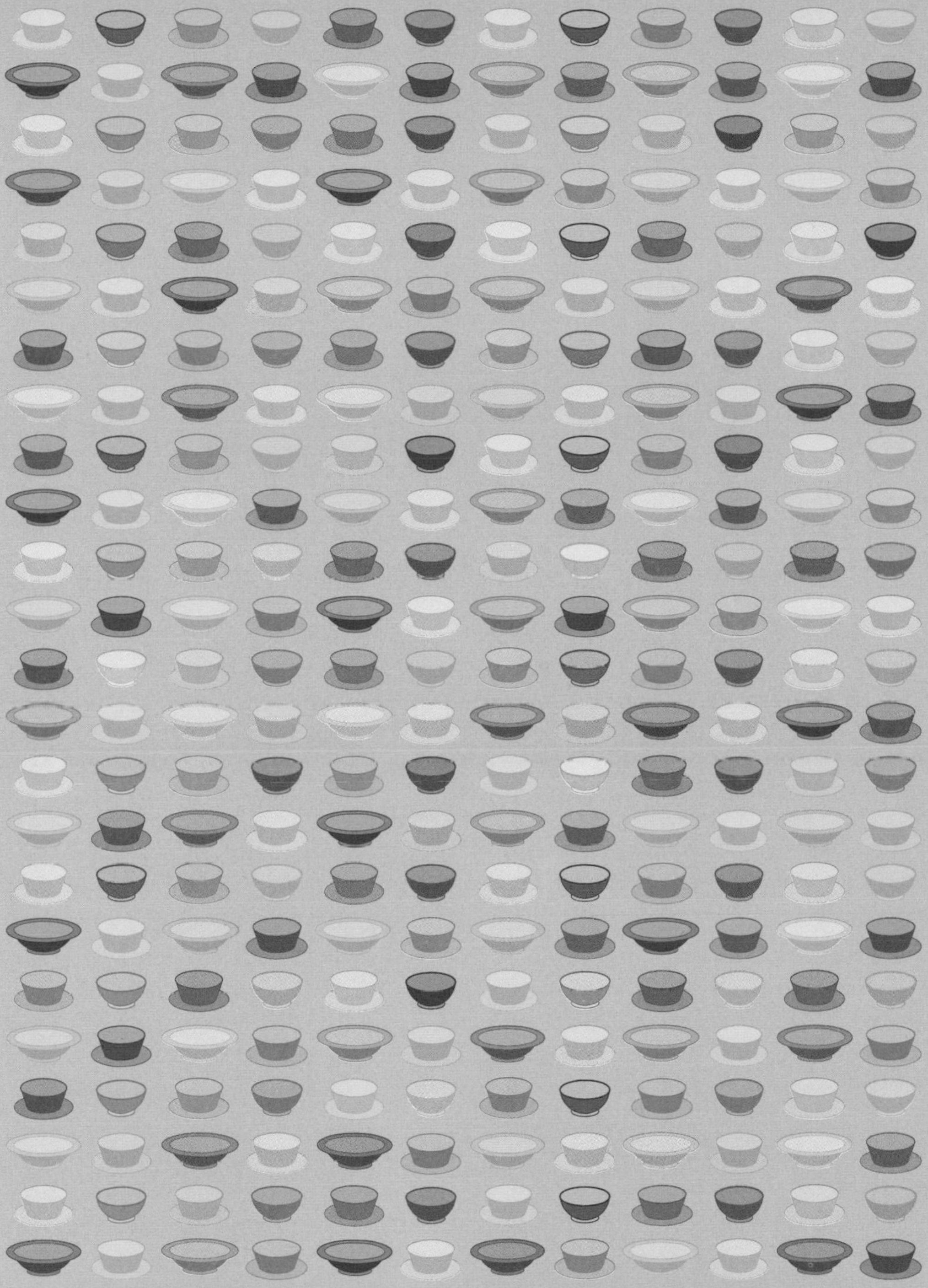

Penguin
Random
House

Writer Kate Turner

Senior Editor Ruth O'Rourke-Jones

Senior Art Editor Alison Gardner

Nutritionist Joy Skipper

Jacket Designer Harriet Yeomans

Jacket Editor Libby Brown

Pre-production Producer
Catherine Williams

Print Producer Stephanie McConnell

Creative Technical Support
Sonia Charbonnier

Photography Will Heap

Managing Editor Dawn Henderson

Managing Art Editor
Marianne Markham

Art Director Maxine Pedliham

Publishing Director Mary-Clare Jerram

DK US

Editor Christy Lusiak

Managing Editor Lori Cates Hand

Publisher Mike Sanders

Every effort has been made to ensure that the
information in this book is complete and accurate.
However, neither the publisher nor the author is
engaged in rendering professional advice or services to
the individual reader. The ideas, procedures, and
suggestions contained in this book are not intended as
a substitute for consulting with your healthcare
provider. All matters regarding your heath require
medical supervision. Neither the publishers nor the
author shall be liable or responsible for any loss or
damage allegedly arising from any information or
suggestion in this book.

First American Edition, 2016

Published in the United States by
DK Publishing, 345 Hudson Street,
New York, New York 10014

Copyright © 2016 Dorling Kindersley Ltd.
DK, a Division of Penguin Random
House LLC

16 17 18 19 20   10 9 8 7 6 5 4 3 2 1

001 – 299214 – Dec/16

All rights reserved.
Without limiting the rights under the copyright
reserved above, no part of this publication may be
reproduced, stored in or introduced into a retrieval
system, or transmitted, in any form, or by any means
(electronic, mechanical, photocopying, recording,
or otherwise), without the prior written permission
of the copyright owner.

Published in Great Britain by
Dorling Kindersley Limited.

A catalog record for this book is available from the
Library of Congress.

ISBN: 978-1-4654-5877-3

DK books are available at special discounts when
purchased in bulk for sales promotions, premiums,
fund-raising, or educational use. For details, contact:
DK Publishing Special Markets, 345 Hudson Street,
New York, New York 10014 SpecialSales@dk.com

Printed and bound in China

All images © Dorling Kindersley Limited

For further information see: www.dkimages.com

A WORLD OF IDEAS:
SEE ALL THERE IS TO KNOW
www.dk.com

POWERbowls

ALL YOU NEED IN ONE HEALTHY BOWL

Contents

Breakfast
page 16

Quinoa & berry
porridge
page 18

Black rice
& tropical fruit bowl
page 20

Savory oatmeal
power bowl
page 22

Ancient grains
porridge with pear
page 26

 *Oatmeal bowls* **page 24**

Acai berry & kale
smoothie bowl
page 28

Raw buckwheat &
blueberry bowl
page 30

Lunch on the go
page 32

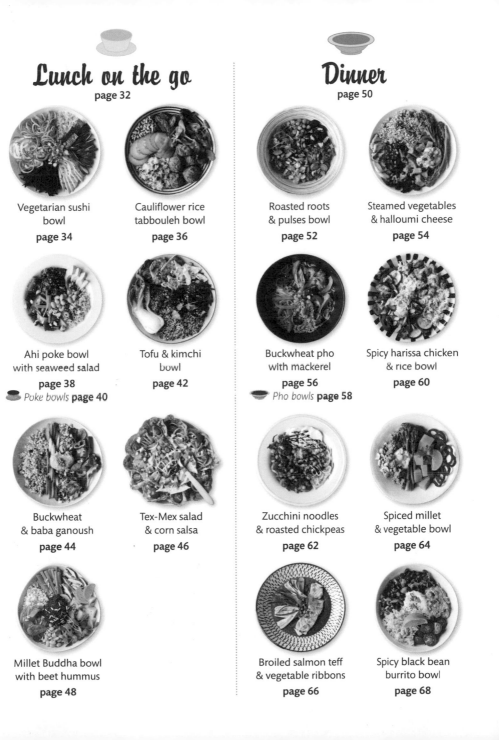

Vegetarian sushi
bowl
page 34

Cauliflower rice
tabbouleh bowl
page 36

Ahi poke bowl
with seaweed salad
page 38
Poke bowls **page 40**

Tofu & kimchi
bowl
page 42

Buckwheat
& baba ganoush
page 44

Tex-Mex salad
& corn salsa
page 46

Millet Buddha bowl
with beet hummus
page 48

Dinner
page 50

Roasted roots
& pulses bowl
page 52

Steamed vegetables
& halloumi cheese
page 54

Buckwheat pho
with mackerel
page 56
Pho bowls **page 58**

Spicy harissa chicken
& rice bowl
page 60

Zucchini noodles
& roasted chickpeas
page 62

Spiced millet
& vegetable bowl
page 64

Broiled salmon teff
& vegetable ribbons
page 66

Spicy black bean
burrito bowl
page 68

What is a power bowl?

A power bowl is a nutritionally complete and totally balanced meal in one bowl. Whether it's a quick and easy breakfast for the family, a workday lunch for one, or a leisurely weekend dinner with friends, these bowls are full of flavor, bursting with color, and wonderfully simple.

Here's how

Take one beautiful bowl, fill it with super-healthy ingredients, and make it look amazing. Then sit back and enjoy eating a meal that's packed with nutrient-dense foods and tons of natural energy to help power you through your day.

Superfood ingredients

All the recipes in this book focus on fresh fruits and vegetables, healthy whole grains, lean proteins, nuts, seeds, and nutri-boosting superfoods. They are naturally free of gluten and refined sugars with lots of variations to

Color—pile on fruit
and vegetables for lots of
vitamins and minerals

Base—grains
and pulses to keep
you energized

Crunch—nuts and
seeds for extra
protein and texture

inspire you and help you make the
recipes your own. Eating this way can
bring awesome health benefits, including
increased energy levels, improved moods,
and greater ability to concentrate, and
may even help you get a better night's
sleep to leave you feeling recharged. Every
delicious power bowl recipe is packed full
of superfood vitality to make you feel
fantastic and fill you with "get up and go"!

Protein—keeps you feeling full
and helps your body repair

"...a nutritionally complete
& totally balanced meal in one bowl..."

Building a **power bowl**

There are so many ways to create the perfect power bowl. Layer up with grains, veggies, nuts, seeds, tasty dressings, and a power-packed protein source for a balanced and complete meal in one bowl. Choose the best-quality—preferably organic—ingredients for maximum health and vitality.

1. Base   2. Protein   3. Veg and fruit

Start with a high-energy base layer, such as the lentils used here. Whole grains, pulses, and noodles are awesome.

+

Add protein-rich chickpeas (as above), fish, eggs, or tofu. Mixing grains and pulses provides a complete plant-based protein.

+

Pile on colorful raw or cooked veggies, such as carrots, kale, beet, sweet potato, celeriac, and arugula—all full of vitamins.

"Presoak pulses, grains, nuts, and seeds to maximize their nutritional benefits."

Sunday prep
Read the recipes thoroughly and plan ahead. Make dressings, soak, chop, and marinate over the weekend to save time during a busy week.

4. Crunchy toppings

5. Dressing

+ Add extra crunch and texture with a sprinkling of nuts and seeds, such as walnuts and pumpkin seeds.

+ Finish off with a dressing. This one is made from honey, olive oil, and whole-grain mustard.

= **Dig in and power up!**

Power ingredients

The best way to ensure a great-tasting power bowl is to use quality ingredients. Source fresh, seasonal, local, and organic produce for maximum benefits. These are some of our favorite nutrient-dense superfood ingredients.

Grains & pulses

Amaranth Rich in vitamins A and C, fiber, calcium, potassium, iron, and all nine essential amino acids, amaranth can protect against heart disease and lower blood pressure.

Beans and peas When combined with a grain, such as brown rice, beans and peas provide a complete plant-protein source that is on a par with meat.

Buckwheat Gluten-free buckwheat has high levels of vitamins, minerals, and fiber. It keeps the body fueled with slow-release energy.

Lentils A great source of plant protein, lentils are also high in fiber, magnesium, potassium, and folate.

Millet Packed with magnesium, copper, manganese, and phosphorous, millet can help protect against Type 2 diabetes and support digestive health.

Oats One of the best sources of soluble fiber, oats help to lower cholesterol and leave you feeling energized for hours.

Quinoa Containing all the essential amino acids our bodies need, quinoa is loaded with manganese, magnesium, and phosphorous, all vital for well-being.

Rice, black and brown Whole grains such as rice can help reduce the risk of heart disease. Brown rice is rich in selenium and manganese, while black rice is packed with antioxidants.

Teff The tiny grain with a big nutrient hit, teff has more calcium than any other grain and eight of the nine amino acids essential for muscle recovery and repair.

Tofu, tempeh, and miso Made from soybeans and fermented to maximize their health benefits, these foods are high in complete proteins that contain all of the body's essential amino acids.

Nuts & seeds

Almonds Loaded with more vitamin E than any other nut, plus bone-friendly calcium, versatile almonds can be sliced, ground, left whole, or even made into milk.

Cashews An abundant source of essential minerals, such as manganese, potassium, iron, magnesium, and zinc.

Chia seeds These tiny seeds contain high levels of omega-3 fatty acids and have five times more calcium than cow's milk. They are rich in antioxidants, anti-inflammatories, and energy-enhancing fiber.

Flaxseeds (linseeds) These are one of the best plant-based sources of omega-3 fatty acids and are high in B vitamins.

Hemp seeds This source of veggie protein helps to regulate energy levels. Hemp seeds are packed with zinc, magnesium, and calcium and are a powerful anti-inflammatory.

Macadamia nuts Packed with healthy fats, these nuts are high in thiamine, manganese, and copper.

Pumpkin seeds These are a source of tryptophan, which is converted by the body into a sleep-regulating neurotransmitter, serotonin.

Sesame seeds Full of vitamins, minerals, and phytosterols that aid the immune system, sesame seeds also help to regulate cholesterol and may even help to fight cancer.

Sunflower seeds Packed full of essential amino acids, these seeds are also a rich source of folic acid.

Walnuts Packing a massive protein punch, walnuts are particularly high in cholesterol-lowering compounds, as well as the stress-busting hormone melatonin.

Fruit

Avocado Full of antioxidants, avocados are high in healthy fats, fiber, potassium, vitamin E, and magnesium. They are great for skin.

Banana Rich in potassium and easy to digest, bananas are said to provide instant energy, stabilize blood pressure, and lift depression.

Blueberries and blackberries Filled with antioxidants, fiber, vitamin C, and cancer-fighting compounds, these berries are thought to be good for the heart and to boost eyesight and memory.

Coconut With potent antibacterial, antifungal, and antimicrobial properties, coconut is the richest natural source of lauric acid, which boosts immunity and fights disease.

Goji berries Containing more beta-carotene than any other plant, goji berries also have more iron, gram for gram, than steak.

Lemon and lime Both excellent sources of vitamin C and citric acid, which can aid digestion.

Mango High in amino acids and A and B vitamins, mangoes have antioxidant compounds that are thought to protect against cancer.

Pomegranate Full of potent antioxidants that can protect against heart disease and cancer, this fruit is rich in vitamins A, C, and E.

Tomato Contains lycopene, a powerful antioxidant that may help

to protect against cancer, and choline, a nutrient that aids sleep, muscle movement, and memory.

Vegetables

Beets Known to lower blood pressure and thought to be a potent detoxifier, beets also support heart health.

Broccoli Protein-rich broccoli is full of vitamins and antioxidants, plus compounds that fight illness, improve reproductive health, and reduce the risk of heart disease.

Carrot Exceptionally high in vitamin A and beta-carotene, carrots are one of the most powerful antioxidants on earth.

Garlic This contains allicin, which has antibacterial, antifungal, and antiviral properties.

Mushrooms All mushrooms are loaded with essential nutrients—many are high in selenium and vitamin D, and shiitake mushrooms contain beta-glucans that boost immune system health.

Red cabbage Rich in a potent antioxidant called anthocyanin, red cabbage is said to support the health of the heart and circulation.

Seaweed Nutrient-rich, low-calorie seaweed is a potent source of iodine, vital for thyroid function.

Spinach Spinach is high in iron, protein, and vitamin C, and rich in beta-carotene for skin health.

Sweet potato A source of fiber, antioxidants, and vitamins A, C, and B, sweet potato helps regulate blood-sugar levels and supports skin health.

Other great ingredients

Apple cider vinegar An ancient folk remedy, this vinegar has insulin-regulating properties that help lower blood-sugar levels.

Cilantro A source of vitamins K, A, and C, cilantro leaves and seeds have antioxidant properties.

Dairy Plain yogurts and cheeses are high in bone and tooth-friendly calcium, while probiotics support the digestive and immune system.

Eggs High in protein with 20 amino acids in an easily digestible form, eggs provide every vitamin except vitamin C. A good source of omega-3 fatty acids, essential for a healthy heart and nervous system.

Lean meat Chicken and fish are high in complex proteins, which support muscle recovery and repair.

Oily fish are rich in omega-3 fatty acids, which are essential for heart health and for preventing inflammatory diseases.

Olive oil Rich in monounsaturated fatty acids, renowned for their cholesterol-balancing properties.

Raw honey With antibacterial, antifungal, and antiviral properties, raw honey is a powerful natural antioxidant and healer.

Tamari soy sauce A gluten-free soy sauce that provides niacin, manganese, and the mood-enhancing amino acid, tryptophan.

Turmeric A powerful anti-inflammatory and immune booster, turmeric has been used for centuries in Chinese and Indian medicine.

Hummus

Cashew Cream

Hazelnut Dukkah

Beet Hummus

Make it or buy it!

These simple favorites add flavor and texture to many of the recipes in the book. You can easily buy them, but homemade is always the best.

Hazelnut Dukkah

Makes approx. ¾ cup
½ cup hazelnuts • ¼ cup sesame seeds • 1 tbsp coriander (cilantro seeds) • 1 tbsp cumin seeds • 1 tsp salt • 1 tsp pepper

1 Preheat the oven to 350°F (180°C). Roast the hazelnuts on a baking sheet in the oven for 10 minutes.
2 Once cool, rub the nuts to loosen the skins. Put the nuts, seeds, salt, and pepper in a food processor and pulse until finely chopped. Store in an airtight container in the fridge for up to 2 months.

Hummus

Makes approx. 1¼ cups
¾ cup chickpeas, ready to eat • 2 tbsp lemon juice • 1 clove garlic, crushed • 1 tbsp tahini • ½ tsp salt • 2 tbsp olive oil • 1–3 tbsp filtered water (optional) • Salt and pepper to taste

1 Put all the ingredients, except the oil and water, in a blender and pulse.
2 With the motor running, drizzle in the oil, then the water, until the desired consistency is reached.
3 Season to taste with more lemon, salt, and pepper. Store in an airtight container in the fridge for 2–3 days.

Beet Hummus

Makes approx. 1½ cups
¾ cup beets, coarsely chopped • ½ tbsp olive oil

Place the beets in a roasting pan and drizzle with ½ tbsp of oil. Roast for 30 minutes until soft. Follow from Step 1 in hummus recipe (see left).

Cashew Cream

Makes approx. ¾ cup
1 cup cashews • ½ cup filtered water

1 Soak cashews overnight in double the volume of water. Drain and rinse.

Granola

Sweet Potato Falafels

Pickled Cucumber

2 Put the cashews in a blender with the filtered water and pulse until smooth. Store in the fridge in an airtight container for 2–3 days.

Granola

Makes approx. 3¼ cups

½ cup rolled oats · ⅔ cup pumpkin seeds · ½ cup sunflower seeds · 2 tbsp chia seeds · ¼ cup walnuts · ¼ cup whole almonds · 1 tsp cinnamon · 1 tbsp coconut oil · 1 tbsp maple syrup · 3 dates, pitted and chopped · ¼ cup goji berries

I Preheat the oven to 350°F (180°C).
2 Combine the oats, seeds, nuts, and cinnamon in a big bowl.
3 Heat the coconut oil and syrup in a pan, then stir this into the dry mixture.
4 Line a baking sheet with parchment paper, spread out the granola mixture, and bake in the oven for 10 minutes.
5 Remove from the oven, stir well,

and return to the oven for another 10 minutes, until golden.
6 Remove from oven and stir in the dried fruit. Let cool. Store in an airtight container for up to 3 months.

Sweet Potato Falafels

Makes 4

½ cup sweet potato, skin on and diced · 1 tsp coconut oil · 1 tbsp red onion, finely chopped · 1 garlic clove, crushed · ¼ tsp turmeric · ¼ tsp cumin · ½ tsp red chile pepper, finely chopped · ¼ cup chickpeas, ready to eat · 1 tbsp lemon juice · ½ tbsp tahini · 1 tbsp cilantro, chopped · Salt and pepper to taste

I Preheat the oven to 400°F (200°C).
2 Steam the sweet potato for 10–15 minutes until soft.
3 Heat the oil in a frying pan over medium heat and cook the onions and garlic until soft. Add the spices, then cook for 2 minutes.

4 Put the chickpeas, potato, lemon juice, tahini, and cilantro in a food processor and pulse until very roughly combined. Transfer to a bowl with the spicy onion mixture and combine.
5 Season with salt and pepper.
6 Roll the mix into four balls, put on a baking pan, and bake for 20 minutes.
7 Let cool on a wire rack to firm up before serving.

Pickled Cucumber

Makes approx. 2 cups

1 cucumber · 1 tsp salt · 1 tsp red chile, seeded, finely chopped · 1 tbsp fresh ginger, peeled and finely chopped · ½ cup apple cider vinegar · 1 tbsp raw honey

I Slice the cucumber into strips along its length, making ribbons.
2 Combine all the ingredients in a large bowl. Stir well, cover, and refrigerate for between 30 minutes and 2 hours, while it pickles.
3 Transfer to a glass jar and store in the fridge for up to 2 months.

Kimchi

Chimichurri Sauce

Corn Salsa

Baba Ganoush

Kimchi

Fills an approx. 1-quart (1-liter) jar
3 cups (25fl oz) filtered water •
3 tbsp salt • 6½ cups (16oz) red
cabbage, shredded • ¾ cup daikon
(or red) radish, julienned • 1 red
chile, seeded, coarsely chopped • 3
garlic cloves, crushed • 3 tbsp ginger,
grated • 2 green onions, chopped

1 Sterilize your jar and lid in boiling
water. Let dry.
2 Mix the water and salt in a jug.
3 Put the cabbage and radish in a
bowl and cover it with the salty water.
4 Place a plate directly on top of the
cabbage mix to keep it immersed in
brine. Cover with plastic wrap. Let
stand overnight at room temperature.
5 Drain the cabbage and radish,
reserving the brine. Rinse under cold
running water and return to the bowl.
6 Add the chile, garlic, ginger, and
green onions to the bowl and mix
well with the cabbage. Pack the
mixture firmly into the jar by pushing
it down with the back of a spoon.
7 Pour the reserved brine into the
jar until the mixture is just covered.

8 Pop the lid on and leave at room
temperature, out of direct sunlight,
for 1–5 days.
9 Remove the lid each day and push
the mix back down under the brine.
It's ready when you like the taste!
10 Kimchi can be eaten immediately
or left to develop its distinctive
flavor—deliciously tangy. When it's
right for your tastebuds, transfer to the
fridge, where it will keep for up to 1
month in an airtight container.

Baba Ganoush

Makes approx. 1½ cups
1 medium eggplant • 1 garlic clove,
crushed • 1 tbsp lemon juice •
¼ cup tahini • Salt to taste

1 Heat the oven to 425°F (220°C).
Place the eggplant in a baking pan
and prick the skin with a fork. Roast
for 25 minutes.
2 Peel off the skin while hot and
remove the stem, then roughly chop
the flesh. Put in a food processor with
the garlic, lemon, and tahini. Blend to
a thick purée. Add salt and lemon
juice to taste. Let cool.

Chimichurri Sauce

Makes approx. ½ cup
4 garlic cloves, crushed • ¾ cup
parsley, chopped • 2 tsp dried
oregano • 3 tbsp apple cider
vinegar • 4–6 tbsp olive oil

1 Add the ingredients (except the oil)
to the small bowl of a food processor
or blender. Pulse until combined.
2 With the motor running, drizzle in
the oil until smooth. Store in an
airtight container in the fridge for up
to 2 weeks. Shake well before serving.

Corn Salsa

Makes approx. ½ cup
1 tbsp coconut oil • 1 corn on the
cob • ¼ red onion, finely sliced •
1 large tomato, diced • 1 tsp red
chile, seeded and finely chopped •
juice of ½ lime • 1 tbsp cilantro,
chopped • 1 tsp olive oil • Salt
and pepper to taste

1 Heat the oil in a frying pan over
high heat. Place the corn in the pan
and cook until it is just starting to char,
turning frequently.

Harissa Marinade

Guacamole

Balsamic Glaze

Avocado Pesto

Salsa Verde

2 Remove and let cool before slicing the kernels off the cob.
3 Add the corn to a bowl with the remaining salsa ingredients, then season with salt and pepper. It is best eaten fresh, but can be stored in the fridge for 1–2 days.

Harissa Marinade

Makes approx. ½ cup
1 red bell pepper, roasted and peeled • 1 tsp cumin seeds • 1 tsp caraway seeds • 1 tbsp olive oil • 1 tbsp lemon juice • 2 garlic cloves, crushed • 1 tsp apple cider vinegar • ¼ tsp salt • ¼ tsp chile flakes (to taste)

1 Heat the oven to 425°F (220°C). Put the red pepper on a small baking sheet and roast for 10–15 minutes, until soft and the skin is blistering. Remove and let cool before peeling. Discard the skin and put the flesh and seeds in the small bowl of a food processor.
2 Add the rest of the ingredients and blend until smooth. Store in an airtight container in the fridge for up to 1 week.

Guacamole

Makes approx. 1 cup
⅔ cup avocado flesh • ½ cup tomato, cored and chopped • 1 tbsp lime juice • ½–1 tsp red chile, seeded and finely chopped • 1 garlic clove, crushed • 1 tbsp cilantro, chopped • 1 pinch of salt

1 Put the ingredients in the small bowl of a food processor and pulse until roughly combined. Keep it chunky!
2 Alternatively, place the avocado in a bowl and mash with a fork. Coarsely chop the tomato into small pieces. Add all the other ingredients to the bowl and combine.
3 Best eaten fresh, but can be stored in an airtight container in the fridge overnight.

Balsamic Glaze

Makes approx. ½–¼ cup
1 cup balsamic vinegar

1 Pour the vinegar into a small saucepan and bring to a boil.
2 Turn down the heat and simmer, uncovered, for 10–15 minutes, until

the vinegar has reduced to around a quarter in volume, but is still runny.
3 Store in an airtight container for up to 6 months.

Salsa Verde

Makes approx. 1 cup
1¾ cups cilantro • 1 cup cashews • 4 tbsp lime juice • 1 garlic clove, crushed • ⅓ cup (2½fl oz) water • ¼ tsp salt • 1 tbsp olive oil

1 Place the ingredients (except the oil) in a blender. Blend until combined.
2 With the motor running, drizzle the oil in until smooth. Store in an airtight container in the fridge for 1 week.

Avocado Pesto

Makes approx. ¾ cup
⅔ cup avocado flesh • 2 tbsp pine nuts • 2 tsp lime juice • 1 garlic clove, crushed • 4 tsp olive oil • 1 cup cilantro • Salt to taste

Combine the ingredients in a food processor or blender and whizz until smooth. Store in an airtight container in the fridge for 1–2 days.

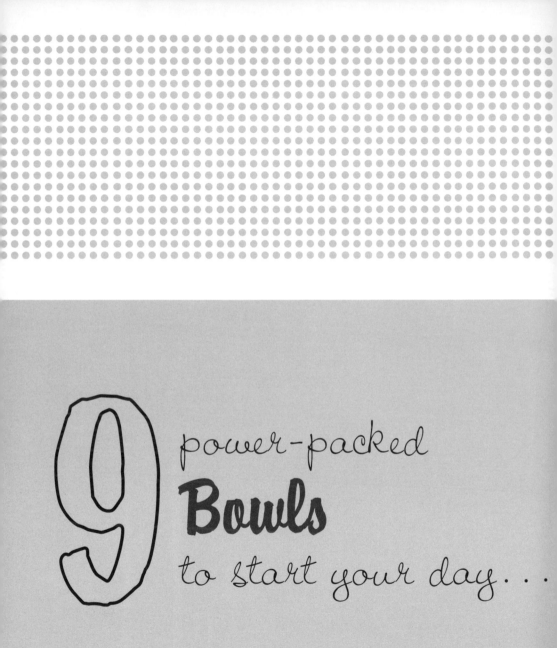

9 power-packed **Bowls** to start your day . . .

Breakfast

Quinoa & berry porridge

Protein and antioxidant packed, this porridge keeps you energized until lunch.

Ingredients

Serves 1

¼ cup tricolor quinoa

1 cup almond milk

Maple syrup or raw honey to taste

2 tbsp blueberries

¼ cup raspberries

¼ cup blackberries

1 tbsp dried goji berries

1 tbsp almond slices

1 tsp golden flaxseeds (linseeds)

1 pinch of ground cinnamon

1 tbsp acai berry powder (optional)

Method

1 To make the quinoa porridge, rinse the quinoa and place in a pan on the stove. Add the almond milk, then bring to a boil.

2 Turn down the heat and simmer, uncovered, for around 25 minutes until the liquid has been absorbed, stirring occasionally.

3 Add maple syrup or honey to taste.

4 Place in a bowl and top with the berries, nuts, and seeds.

5 Sprinkle with a pinch of cinnamon. Add a spoonful of acai berry powder, if desired.

Boost it!

For a mega-antioxidant boost, mix 1 tbsp acai berry powder with your cooked quinoa.

Per serving:

Calories 522 · **Total fat** 31.1g · **Sat. fat** 7.8g · **Protein** 18.8g · **Carbohydrates** 44.5g · **Sugar** 12.3g · **Sodium** 60mg · **Fiber** 16.1g

Sunday prep

Make your quinoa porridge ahead and store for up to 4 days in the fridge. Simply warm through in a pan before adding toppings.

Black rice
& tropical fruit bowl

Coconut contains lauric acid, which boosts "good" HDL cholesterol levels in the blood.

Ingredients

Serves 1

¼ cup black rice

1oz (30g) coconut flakes
(or dessicated coconut)

¾ cup warm water

1 tsp vanilla extract

1 tbsp maple syrup to taste

1 tsp baobab powder (optional)

½ small pineapple, cored and diced,
approx. ⅓ cup

¼ mango, sliced

1 passionfruit, scooped out

½ kiwi, sliced

1 tbsp macadamia nuts, lightly
toasted and crushed

1 tbsp goji berries

1 tbsp coconut flakes, lightly
toasted

1 tbsp cashew cream
(optional: see p.12)

Method

1 Soak the rice overnight in double the volume of water. Drain and rinse.

2 To make the coconut "milk", put the coconut flakes and warm water in a high-speed blender and let sit for 5 minutes, then blend until smooth and milky.

3 Using cheesecloth, line a strainer, and strain the milk over a jug.

4 Place ⅔ cup of homemade coconut milk, the rice, and vanilla extract in a saucepan on the stove and bring to a boil. Reduce the heat and simmer, covered, for 30–40 minutes until the rice is soft, yet chewy, and most of the liquid has been absorbed.

5 Add maple syrup and extra coconut milk to taste, plus baobab powder if using.

6 Load up your bowl with the rice, tropical fruits, macadamia nuts, goji berries, and toasted coconut flakes. Drizzle with cashew cream, if using.

Make it!

Cashew cream
on p.12

Buy it!

Per serving:

Calories 812 · **Total fat** 46g · **Sat. fat** 24.2g · **Protein** 12g
Carbohydrates 94.7g · **Sugar** 49.2g · **Sodium** 94mg · **Fiber** 16.8g

Sunday prep

Make the coconut milk in advance and store in an airtight container in the fridge for 2–3 days. Shake well before using. The pulp is great in smoothies.

Savory oatmeal
power bowl

Oats are full of slow-release energy that will keep you satisfied for hours.

Ingredients

Serves 1

½ cup rolled oats
½ tsp ground turmeric
½ cup almond milk
½ cup filtered water
1 pinch of salt
¾ cup red cabbage, shredded
¼ cup black beans
1 handful of baby spinach
½ avocado, peeled and sliced
1–2 tsp hazelnut dukkah (see p.12)
Salt and pepper to taste
Sesame oil (optional)

Method

1 Combine the oats in a saucepan on the stove with the turmeric, almond milk, water, and salt. Bring to a boil, then turn down the heat and simmer, uncovered, for 5–7 minutes until the liquid has been absorbed. Take the pan off the heat and set aside.

2 Place the red cabbage and beans in the top of a steaming pan. Steam on the stove for 5 minutes.

3 Stir the spinach into the oatmeal, cover, and leave to wilt for around 5 minutes.

4 Place the turmeric and spinach oatmeal in a bowl and top with the cabbage, beans, avocado, and dukkah.

5 Season with salt and pepper, then drizzle with sesame oil, if desired.

Sunday prep

Make your dukkah (see p.12) in advance and store in an airtight container in the fridge for up to 2 months.

Per serving:
Calories 578 · **Total fat** 30.6g · **Sat. fat** 5.5g · **Protein** 19.4g ·
Carbohydrates 61g · **Sugar** 8.9g · **Sodium** 232mg · **Fiber** 18.1g

Make it!
Hazelnut dukkah
on p. 12
Buy it!

Oatmeal *bowls*

Starting your day with a bowlful of oats is a great way to make sure you stay energized all morning. Oats are one of the best sources of soluble fiber, which helps to keep you feeling full and avoid snacking.

Beet & apple

Ingredients

½ cup rolled oats • ½ cup almond milk • 4¼fl oz (125ml) filtered water • ½ apple, skin on, grated • 1 tbsp hemp seeds • 1 tsp beet powder or 1 tbsp beet juice • Raw honey to taste • 1 tsp pistachios, lightly crushed • 1 tsp pumpkin seeds • 1 tsp sunflower seeds • 1 tbsp pomegranate seeds

Method

1 Combine the oats, almond milk, filtered water, apple, hemp seeds, and beet powder in a saucepan and bring to a boil.

2 Turn down the heat and simmer, uncovered, for around 5 minutes until the liquid has been absorbed, stirring occasionally. Add more milk if you like it runnier.

3 Add honey to taste.

4 Place the oatmeal in a bowl and top with the nuts and seeds.

Per serving:
Calories 440 • Total fat 23.6g • Sat. fat 2.5g
Protein 17.9g • Carbohydrates 39.1g
Sugar 15.9g • Sodium 33mg • Fiber 7.6g

Tempeh & tomato

Ingredients

½ tbsp tamari soy sauce • 1 tbsp olive oil • ½ tsp Sriracha sauce • 1 garlic clove, crushed • ¼ tsp ground cumin • ½ cup tempeh, sliced • 1 tomato, chopped • 2 mushrooms, sliced • ½ cup rolled oats • ¾ cup water • 1 tbsp hummus • 1 pinch of cayenne pepper • 1 handful of arugula • 1 tbsp sliced almonds, toasted • Salt and pepper to taste

Method

1 Mix together the tamari soy sauce, 1 tsp olive oil, Sriracha, garlic, and cumin. Add the tempeh. Marinate for 5 minutes.

2 Heat the rest of the oil in a pan over medium heat. Add the mushrooms, chopped tomato, and marinated tempeh. Cook until the vegetables are starting to soften.

3 Add the oats and water to a pan. Simmer for 5 minutes, stirring. Remove from the heat. Stir in hummus, a pinch of salt, and cayenne pepper.

4 Pour the oatmeal into a bowl and top with the vegetables, tempeh, arugula, and toasted almond slices. Season with salt and pepper and drizzle with olive oil.

Per serving:
Calories 526 • Total fat 31.8g • Sat. fat 3.6g
Protein 24.2g • Carbohydrates 36.4g
Sugar 8.5g • Sodium 342mg • Fiber 10.3g

Amaranth & egg

Ingredients

¼ cup amaranth • ¼ cup rolled oats • ½ cup almond milk • ⅔ cup (5fl oz) water • 1 pinch of salt • 6 asparagus spears, trimmed • 1 free-range egg • 1 small handful microgreens • 1 tsp olive oil • 1–2 tsp hazelnut dukkah (see p.12)

Method

1 Rinse the amaranth and put it in a pan on the stove with the oats, almond milk, water, and salt. Bring to a boil, reduce the heat, and simmer, covered, for 20 minutes until the liquid absorbs. Stir occasionally, adding more water if needed.

2 Steam the asparagus for 3–5 minutes until al dente.

3 Bring a pan of water to a boil, reduce to a simmer, and crack the egg into it. Poach for 2–4 minutes.

4 Pour the amaranth mix into a bowl. Top with the asparagus, egg, and microgreens. Drizzle with oil and sprinkle with dukkah.

Per serving:
Calories 441 • Total fat 20.4g • Sat. fat 12g
Protein 22.7g • Carbohydrates 40.8g
Sugar 5.2g • Sodium 280mg • Fiber 8g

Ancient grains
porridge with pear

Rich in phytonutrients, these ancient supergrains are high in protein for sustained energy.

Ingredients

Serves 1

1 tbsp millet

1 tbsp amaranth

1 tbsp buckwheat groats

1 tbsp quinoa

¾ cup almond milk, plus extra
if desired

1 small ripe pear, peeled and cored

1 tbsp pomegranate seeds

1 tbsp pistachios, crushed

1 tbsp cashew cream
(optional: see p.12)

1 pinch of cinnamon

Raw honey to taste

Method

1 Combine the grains and soak overnight in double the volume of water. In the morning, drain and rinse well.

2 Place the grains in a saucepan with the milk. Bring to a boil, then turn down the heat and simmer gently for 15 minutes, stirring occasionally, until most of the milk is absorbed and the grains are soft—these grains have more texture and are more al dente than oats.

3 Add some more milk if you like your porridge a little runnier.

4 Roughly mash half the pear with a fork and stir through the porridge. Cut the remaining pear into chunks.

5 Place the porridge in a bowl and top with the chunks of pear, pomegranate seeds, pistachios, a drizzle of cashew cream, and a pinch of cinnamon.

6 Sweeten with raw honey to taste.

Per serving:
Calories 383 · Total fat 13.8g · Sat. fat 1.7g · Protein 10.5g ·
Carbohydrates 55.6g · Sugar 14.1g · Sodium 103mg · Fiber 6.6g

Make it!
Cashew cream
on p.12
Buy it!

Acai berry & kale
smoothie bowl

With kale, acai berries, and chia seeds, this bowl is full of anti-aging antioxidants.

Ingredients

Serves 1

⅓ cup frozen blackberries

⅓ cup frozen blueberries

¼ cup kale, destalked and chopped

⅓ cup banana, chopped

⅓ cup nut milk, or more depending on thickness desired

1 tbsp acai berry powder

1 tbsp flaxseed powder

1 tbsp chia seeds

Raw honey to taste

2–3 tbsp granola (see p.13)

1 handful of blackberries

1 strawberry, sliced

⅓ cup banana, sliced

1 sprig of mint (optional)

Method

1 Put all the ingredients, except the honey and toppings, in a high-speed blender or food processor and blend until smooth. You may need to push the mixture down with a wooden spoon. It should be quite thick and spoonable.

2 Add raw honey to taste.

3 Transfer to a big bowl and top with granola, berries, banana, and mint, if using.

Make it!

Granola
on p.13

Buy it!

Per serving:
Calories 641 · Total fat 37.4g · Sat. fat 10.2g · Protein 16.6g ·
Carbohydrates 63.4g · Sugar 38.1g · Sodium 41mg · Fiber 29.2g

Sunday prep

Make your granola (see p.13) in advance and store in an airtight container. Enjoy it with milk, on yogurt, as a snack, or with a smoothie.

Raw buckwheat
& blueberry bowl

Start your day with a bowl of low-GI buckwheat to help prevent blood-sugar spikes.

Ingredients

Serves 1

⅓ cup buckwheat groats

4 tbsp cashew cream (see p.12)

1 tbsp hemp seeds

¾ cup blueberries, plus 1 tbsp for topping

½ tsp vanilla extract

⅓ cup banana, chopped

1 tsp maca powder (optional)

Raw honey to taste

¼ cup raspberries

1 tbsp cashews

½ tsp bee pollen (optional)

Method

1 To make the buckwheat mix, soak the buckwheat overnight in double the volume of water. Drain and rinse under cold water.

2 Place the buckwheat in a high-speed blender or food processor with 2 tbsp cashew cream, the hemp seeds, blueberries, vanilla extract, banana, and maca, if using. Blend until smooth and sweeten to taste with raw honey.

3 Spoon the buckwheat mix into a bowl and swirl the rest of the cashew cream through it.

4 Top with fresh raspberries, blueberries, cashews, and a sprinkle of bee pollen, if using.

Make it!

Cashew cream
on p.12

Buy it!

Per serving:

Calories 827 · Total fat 42.3g · Sat. fat 7.1g · Protein 29.9g ·
Carbohydrates 89.7g · Sugar 32.5g · Sodium 21mg · Fiber 14.5g

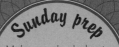

Sunday prep

Make your buckwheat mix ahead and store in an airtight container in the fridge for up to 2 days, ready to be topped with nuts and berries.

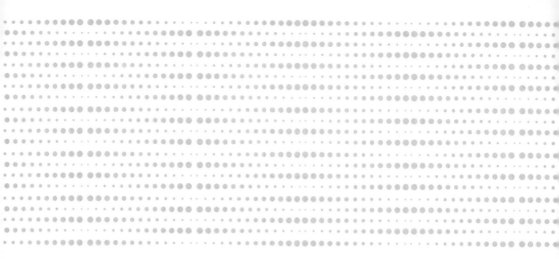

10 cold Bowls to power through the day...

Lunch on the go

Vegetarian sushi bowl

Nutritious raw veggies and carb-rich rice make this an awesome on-the-go lunch.

Ingredients

Serves 1

¼ cup brown basmati rice

1 tbsp olive oil

1 tsp sesame oil

1 tbsp tamari soy sauce

1 tsp honey

1 tbsp balsamic vinegar

1 tbsp ginger, peeled and grated

1 garlic clove, crushed

½ of a medium cucumber

1 large carrot

½ avocado

2oz (60g) beets, grated (about ¾ of a beet)

4 red radishes, sliced

1 small 4x4in (10x10cm) piece of dried nori seaweed, chopped

2 green onions, finely chopped

1 tsp black sesame seeds

Method

1 Rinse the rice and place in a pan on the stove. Cover with water and bring to a boil. Turn down the heat and simmer, covered, for around 30 minutes until soft. Drain, rinse under cold water, and set aside.

2 Prepare the dressing by combining the oils, tamari, honey, vinegar, ginger, and garlic in a small bowl. Whisk and set aside.

3 Leaving the skins on, prepare your vegetables: Create cucumber and carrot "spirals" with a spiralizing machine (or you can grate them if you wish).

4 Peel the avocado and slice the flesh.

5 Arrange the rice, raw vegetables, avocado, and seaweed in a bowl. Sprinkle with green onions and sesame seeds, and drizzle with the tamari and ginger dressing.

Boost it!

For a more intense protein boost, you could add some slices of smoked salmon.

Per serving:

Calories 657 · **Total fat** 37.9g · **Sat. fat** 6.9g · **Protein** 13.8g

Carbohydrates 68.8g · **Sugar** 22.4g · **Sodium** 651mg · **Fiber** 15.5g

Sunday prep

Make the dressing in advance and store in an airtight container in the fridge for up to 2 days.

Cauliflower rice
tabbouleh bowl

Versatile cauliflower makes a great grain-free, low-carb base for this bowl.

Ingredients

Serves 1

6 cherry tomatoes

1 tsp olive oil

Salt and pepper to taste

1¼ cups cauliflower, chopped

1 tsp coconut oil

¼ onion, finely sliced

1 clove garlic, crushed

1 tbsp raisins

1 tbsp cilantro, chopped

1 tbsp pine nuts

½ cup cucumber, sliced

3–4 falafels (store-bought or homemade, see p.13)

1 tbsp pomegranate seeds

DRESSING

1 tbsp olive oil

½ tbsp tahini

½ tbsp lemon juice

Method

1 Preheat the oven to 425°F (220°C).

2 Slice the tomatoes in half, drizzle with oil, and season. Roast them in the oven for 10 minutes, until soft, but holding their shape.

3 Make the "rice" by blending the cauliflower in a food processor.

4 Heat the coconut oil in a large, lidded frying pan on the stove. Add the onion and garlic. Cook for 3–4 minutes, uncovered, until soft.

5 Add the cauliflower with 1 tbsp water, cover, and cook for 4–5 minutes until the cauliflower is softening, but is al dente. Add the raisins and cilantro and stir. Remove from the heat.

6 Toast the pine nuts in a pan for 2–3 minutes until browning.

7 Whisk the dressing ingredients in a small bowl to combine.

8 Place the "rice'" in a bowl. Add the cucumber slices, roasted tomatoes, and falafels. Sprinkle with the toasted nuts and pomegranate seeds, then drizzle with the tahini and lemon dressing. Season with salt and pepper.

Make it!
Falafel
on p. 13
Buy it!

Per serving:

Calories 847 · **Total fat** 60.9g · **Sat. fat** 11.8g · **Protein** 22.3g · **Carbohydrates** 56.8g · **Sugar** 37.7g · **Sodium** 184mg · **Fiber** 15.5g

Sunday prep

Make the cauliflower "rice" in advance and store in an airtight container in the fridge for up to 3–4 days.

Ahi poke bowl
with seaweed salad

Poke is a Hawaiian raw fish salad. This version uses protein-rich ahi (tuna).

Ingredients

Serves 1

1½ tbsp tamari soy sauce (divided)

2 tsp sesame oil (divided)

1 green onion, finely chopped

1 tsp sesame seeds

3½oz (100g) sushi-grade tuna, cut into chunks

1½oz (40g) brown rice

1 tbsp olive oil

1 tsp honey

1 tbsp balsamic vinegar

1 tbsp ginger, grated

1 garlic clove, crushed

1 tbsp dried seaweed (wakame)

¼ cup pickled cucumber (see p.13)

1 small carrot, julienned

1 tbsp edamame (soybeans)

¼ avocado, peeled and sliced

1 tbsp macadamia nuts, toasted

Method

1 To make the marinade, whisk ½ tbsp tamari, 1 tsp sesame oil, the green onion, and sesame seeds in a shallow dish. Add the tuna to the marinade. Cover and chill overnight, or for at least 1 hour.

2 Rinse the rice and place it in a saucepan on the stove. Cover with water and bring to a boil. Lower the heat and simmer, covered, for around 30 minutes until soft. Drain and rinse under cold water.

3 Prepare the dressing by combining 1 tbsp tamari, 1 tsp sesame oil, olive oil, honey, vinegar, ginger, and garlic. Whisk and set aside.

4 Prepare the seaweed as per package instructions. Dried seaweed usually doubles in volume when rehydrated. Drain and chop.

5 Combine the soaked seaweed, cucumber, and carrot in a bowl.

6 Lay a bed of rice in a bowl. Remove the cubes of tuna from the fridge and discard excess marinade. Add the tuna cubes, seaweed and cucumber salad, shelled edamame beans, and avocado to the bowl. Sprinkle with lightly crushed macadamia nuts and drizzle with 2–3 tsp of ginger-soy dressing.

Make it!

Pickled cucumber
on p.13

Buy it!

Per serving:

Calories 735 · Total fat 44.1g · Sat. fat 7.7g · Protein 35g · Carbohydrates 51.8g · Sugar 15.4g · Sodium 1016mg · Fiber 10.5g

Sunday prep

You can marinate
the tuna and store
it overnight, but it
must be eaten the
following day.

Poke
bowls

Traditionally made with marinated raw fish, Hawaiian poke is easily adapted. Vegetarians can replace fish with tofu or mushrooms, and enjoy a bowl full of nutrient-dense veggies and fresh flavors.

Vegetable

Ingredients

¼ cup (2fl oz) fresh lime juice • 1 tbsp apple cider vinegar • 3 tbsp tamari soy sauce • 1 tbsp raw honey • 2 pinches of chile flakes • ½ cup black rice, soaked overnight • 1 tsp olive oil • ¼ cup kale, destalked and chopped • 1 small carrot • ½ small cucumber • 1 large portobello mushroom, cubed • ⅓ cup baby corn, julienned • ¼ avocado, diced • 1 tsp sesame seeds, toasted • 1 green onion, chopped

Method

1 Make the sauce by whisking the lime juice, vinegar, tamari soy sauce, honey, and a pinch of chile flakes. Coat the mushroom with 2 tbsp of sauce. Cover and refrigerate for 1 hour.

2 Place the presoaked rice in a pan and cover with water. Bring to a boil, reduce the heat, and simmer, covered, for 30 minutes until soft. Drain, rinse in cold water, and set aside.

3 Add the oil to the kale. Rub the kale for 2–5 minutes until it softens and turns bright green.

4 Using a vegetable peeler, slice the carrot and cucumber into thin ribbons. Combine with kale.

5 Layer the rice, mushroom, kale salad, corn, and avocado in a bowl. Drizzle with the sauce and top with sesame seeds, green onion, and chile flakes.

Per serving:
Calories 536 • **Total fat** 18.5g • **Sat. fat** 3.1g
Protein 16.6g • **Carbohydrates** 80.7g
Sugar 29.5g • **Sodium** 2,152mg • **Fiber** 9.5g

Salmon

Ingredients

½ tbsp tamari soy sauce • 1 tsp sesame oil • 1 tbsp red onion, finely chopped • 1 green onion, chopped • 1 tsp fresh ginger, grated • 3½oz (100g) sushi-grade salmon fillet, cut into chunks • ¼ cup brown rice • 1 tbsp dried seaweed (arame or hijiki) • ⅓ cup kimchi (see p.14) or raw red cabbage, finely shredded • ¼ cup pickled cucumber (see p.13) or julienned cucumber • 1 tbsp edamame beans • 2 tsp sesame seeds, toasted • 1 sprig of cilantro

Method

1 Whisk the tamari soy sauce, sesame oil, onions, and ginger in a shallow dish. Add the salmon to the marinade and toss to coat the cubes. Cover and refrigerate overnight or for at least 1 hour.

2 Put the rice in a pan, cover with water, and bring to a boil. Reduce the heat and simmer, covered, for 30 minutes until soft. Drain and rinse under cold water.

4 Prepare the seaweed as per package instructions. Dried seaweed needs to be rehydrated and will usually double in volume.

5 Put a bed of rice in a serving bowl. Top with the marinated salmon cubes, kimchi, cucumber, and edamame. Sprinkle with toasted sesame seeds and garnish with seaweed and cilantro.

Per serving:
Calories 489 • **Total fat** 22.9g • **Sat. fat** 3.7g
Protein 31.1g • **Carbohydrates** 40.9g
Sugar 5.7g • **Sodium** 2,029mg • **Fiber** 8.7g

Spicy tofu

Ingredients

¾oz (20g) dried kelp noodles (or seaweed spaghetti) • ½ tbsp tamari soy sauce • 1 tsp sesame oil • 1 pinch chile flakes • 1 tsp fresh ginger, grated or finely chopped • 1 clove garlic, crushed • 1 tbsp onion, finely chopped • 1 small green onion, finely chopped • 1 tsp sesame seeds • 3½oz (100g) tofu (firm, plain), cubed • ½ mango, cubed • 3 tbsp macadamia nuts, toasted and crushed • Sriracha sauce to taste

Method

1 Cook the noodles as per package instructions. Drain, rinse in cold water, and set aside.

2 Combine the tamari soy sauce, sesame oil, chile, ginger, garlic, onions, and sesame seeds and whisk.

3 Place the tofu cubes in the sauce and coat well, taking care not to break the tofu. Let it marinate for around 15 minutes, gently tossing occasionally.

4 Place the noodles in a serving bowl and top with the marinated tofu, mango, and macadamia nuts. Drizzle with any remaining marinade and Sriracha sauce to taste.

Per serving:
Calories 433 • **Total fat** 25.8g • **Sat. fat** 3.6g
Protein 14.5g • **Carbohydrates** 39.5g
Sugar 32.8g • **Sodium** 446mg • **Fiber** 6.9g

Tofu & kimchi bowl

Made with fermented vegetables, kimchi is full of friendly bacteria.

Ingredients

Serves 1

2½ tbsp black beluga lentils
(or green or brown lentils)

2½ tbsp quinoa

3½oz (100g) firm, plain tofu, sliced

1½oz (45g) thick broccoli stem,
sliced widthwise

2 tsp olive oil

2 tsp tamari soy sauce

1½ tsp sesame seeds

2¼oz (65g) mak kimchi (see p.14)

1 baby bok choi, whole

1 sprig of cilantro

1 red radish, sliced

Method

1 Soak the lentils and quinoa in separate jars in double the volume of water and leave overnight. Drain and rinse.

2 Preheat the oven to 400°F (200°C).

3 Place the lentils in a pan on the stove, cover with water, and bring to a boil. Reduce heat and simmer, covered, for 15 minutes. Add the quinoa to the lentils and simmer, covered, for another 10 minutes.

4 Place the tofu slices in one half of a small baking pan and broccoli slices in the other. Drizzle both with olive oil, tamari, and ½ tsp sesame seeds. Put the pan in the oven and bake for 10–15 minutes.

5 Place the bok choi in the top of a steamer pan and steam lightly for 5–8 minutes until tender.

6 Drain the quinoa and lentils and place in a bowl. Top with the kimchi, bok choi, broccoli, and tofu. Garnish with cilantro, the remaining sesame seeds, and slices of radish.

Instead of: **Kimchi**
Switch it!
Steamed cabbage

Per serving:
Calories 398 · **Total fat** 17.3g · **Sat. fat** 2.3g · **Protein** 25.3g
Carbohydrates 37g · **Sugar** 5.9g · **Sodium** 2,079mg · **Fiber** 8.2g

Make it!

Mak kimchi
on p.14

Buy it!

Buckwheat
& baba ganoush

Baba ganoush is a traditional Middle Eastern dip made from fibre-rich eggplant.

Ingredients

Serves 1

⅓ cup buckwheat groats

1 tbsp raisins

1 tbsp parsley, chopped

3 tbsp plain yogurt

1 tbsp lemon juice

Salt and pepper to taste

1 small apple, thinly sliced

3 tbsp sprouted seeds or beans (for example, mung or chickpea)

1 handful of mixed baby salad greens

2 tbsp eggplant baba ganoush (see p.14)

2 tbsp walnuts, coarsely chopped

Method

1 Soak the buckwheat overnight in double the volume of water. Drain, rinse, and place in a saucepan. Cover with water and bring to a boil.

2 Lower the heat and simmer, covered, for 10 minutes until al dente. Drain and place in a mixing bowl.

3 Add the raisins and parsley to the buckwheat and combine.

4 Prepare the dressing by combining the yogurt with lemon juice and a little salt and pepper.

5 Place a bed of buckwheat in a bowl and top with the apple slices, sprouted seeds, and green salad.

6 Finish with a generous dollop of baba ganoush, a sprinkle of walnuts, and a drizzle of yogurt dressing.

7 Season with salt and pepper.

Per serving:
Calories 648 · **Total fat** 33.4g · **Sat. fat** 4.3g · **Protein** 15.1g ·
Carbohydrates 76.4g · **Sugar** 33.7g · **Sodium** 59mg · **Fiber** 7.8g

Make it!

Baba ganoush
on p.14

Buy it!

Tex-Mex salad
& corn salsa

High in protein and fiber, beans make you feel full and keep hunger at bay.

Ingredients

Serves 1

1 tbsp olive oil

¼ small onion, finely sliced

1 garlic clove, crushed

¼ tsp cumin seeds

¼ tsp ground coriander

2 tbsp pinto (or borlotti) beans, ready to eat

1–2 handfuls of lettuce

1 carrot, spiralized (or grated)

1 handful of corn tortilla chips

¼ avocado, peeled and cubed

4 cherry tomatoes, sliced in half

2–4 tbsp corn salsa (see p.14)

1 tbsp cotija (or Parmesan) cheese, grated

2 tbsp chimichurri sauce (see p.14)

Method

1 To make the sauce, gently heat the olive oil in a frying pan on the stove over medium heat. Add the onion and garlic and cook until soft before adding the spices and beans. Heat through for 5–10 minutes until soft, remove from the stove, and set aside.

2 Arrange a bed of lettuce in a bowl and add the carrot, tortilla chips, avocado, tomatoes, and beans.

3 Top with corn salsa and grated cheese.

4 Drizzle with chimichurri sauce.

Sunday prep

Make the sauce and salsa ahead (see p.14). The salsa keeps for 1–2 days, the sauce for 3–4. Store in airtight containers in the fridge.

Per serving:

Calories 444 · Total fat 32.4g · Sat. fat 9.6g · Protein 14.7g · Carbohydrates 25.3g · Sugar 11.7g · Sodium 342mg · Fiber 10.6g

Make it!

Chimichurri sauce
on p.14

Buy it!

Make it!

Corn salsa
on p.14

Buy it!

Millet Buddha bowl
with beet hummus

This bowl is piled with nutrient-rich vegetables and rounded like Buddha's belly!

Ingredients

Serves 1

¼ cup millet

1 cob of corn

1 tbsp olive oil

2 tsp balsamic vinegar

1 small handful of baby spinach

1 handful of pea shoots (or baby salad greens)

3 tbsp cannellini beans, ready to eat

2 cremini or baby portabella mushrooms, sliced

1 small carrot, julienned or grated

½ small mango, peeled and diced

3 tbsp beet hummus (see p.12)

1 tbsp sunflower seeds

2 lime wedges to serve

Salt and pepper to taste

Method

1 Soak the millet overnight in double the volume of water. Drain and rinse well.

2 Place the millet in a saucepan on the stove. Cover with water and bring to a boil. Lower the heat and simmer for 10 minutes until soft but not mushy. Drain and place in a mixing bowl.

3 Using a sharp knife, slice the corn kernels off the cob and combine with the cooked millet.

4 To make the dressing, combine the olive oil and vinegar in a small dish or glass jar and shake well.

5 Put a bed of millet and corn in a bowl and arrange the greens, vegetables, beans, and mango around it with a generous dollop of beet hummus in the middle.

6 Drizzle with dressing, sprinkle with sunflower seeds, and garnish with lime wedges.

7 Season with salt and pepper.

Per serving:
Calories 600 · Total fat 29.1g · Sat. fat 3.7g · Protein 13g · Carbohydrates 71.8g · Sugar 18.8g · Sodium 303mg · Fiber 9.2g

Make it!

Beet hummus
on p. 12

Buy it!

11 energy-balancing **Bowls** to round out your day . . .

51

Dinner

Roasted roots & pulses bowl

Vitamin-packed root vegetables help to lower cholesterol.

Ingredients

Serves 1

1 beet
1 large carrot
¼ bulb celeriac
½ sweet potato
2 tbsp olive oil
½ tsp ground cumin
Salt and pepper to taste
½ cup chickpeas, ready to eat
1 garlic clove, crushed
1 pinch of cayenne pepper
2½ tbsp puy lentils (or green lentils)
2½ tbsp quinoa, rinsed
¼ cup kale leaves, chopped
1 tsp whole-grain mustard
2 tsp raw honey
½ cup arugula
1 tbsp walnut pieces
1 tsp pumpkin seeds

Method

1 Preheat the oven to 400°F (200°C).

2 Leaving the skins on, wash and chop each of the four root vegetables into equal-sized chunks. Place each vegetable in its own quarter of a large roasting pan and drizzle ½ tbsp of the olive oil over the top. Sprinkle with cumin and season with salt and pepper.

3 Mix the chickpeas in a roasting pan with the garlic, ½ tbsp of olive oil, and season with salt and pepper. Place both pans in the oven. Cook the chickpeas for 15 minutes and the vegetables for 25 minutes.

4 Rinse the lentils and put in a pan. Cover with water and bring to a boil. Reduce heat and simmer, covered, for 10 minutes. Add the quinoa and cook for 5 minutes. Steam the kale over the lentils and quinoa for 5 minutes, until it wilts. Drain the lentils and quinoa.

5 Whisk 1 tbsp olive oil, the mustard, and the honey for the dressing.

6 Layer the lentils and quinoa, vegetables, arugula, kale, and chickpeas in a bowl. Top with walnuts, pumpkin seeds, and a drizzle of dressing.

Boost it!

For an extra protein fix and some bone-friendly calcium, crumble ⅓ cup feta cheese over your bowl.

Per serving:
Calories 896 · **Total fat** 56.2g · **Sat. fat** 7.4g · **Protein** 18g
Carbohydrates 85.9g · **Sugar** 50.3g · **Sodium** 508mg · **Fiber** 22.3g

Sunday prep

Roast the chickpeas
ahead and store in the
fridge for 5 days. They
make a tasty protein-
packed snack, so
make a big
batch!

Steamed vegetables & halloumi cheese

Steaming vegetables softens them up but keeps their awesome nutrients intact.

Ingredients

Serves 1

½ sweet potato

1¾oz (50g) broccolini

1½ cups red cabbage, shredded

⅓ cup buckwheat groats

3 tbsp brazil nuts

¾ cup fresh basil, coarsely chopped

3 tbsp olive oil

1 tbsp apple cider vinegar

1 garlic clove, crushed

2–3 tsp coconut oil

4½oz (125g) halloumi cheese, sliced

2 tbsp hummus (see p.12)

1 tsp chia seeds

2 tbsp pomegranate seeds

Method

1 Leaving the skin on, wash and chop the sweet potato into large chunks. Place in a steaming pan and steam for 10 minutes. Add the broccolini and cabbage. Continue steaming the vegetables for 5 minutes (try to keep the vegetables separate), until al dente.

2 Rinse the buckwheat and place in a pan on the stove. Cover with water and bring to a boil. Reduce the heat and simmer, covered, for 10 minutes until soft, but not mushy. Drain and set aside.

3 Prepare the dressing by combining the brazil nuts, basil, olive oil, vinegar, and garlic in the small bowl of a food processor or blender and blend until combined. Set aside.

4 Heat the coconut oil in a griddle pan or skillet to high heat. Put the halloumi slices in the pan and cook for 1 minute on each side.

5 Arrange the buckwheat, steamed vegetables, and halloumi cheese in a bowl and dollop on the hummus.

6 Sprinkle with the chia and pomegranate seeds and drizzle with the brazil nut and basil dressing.

Make it!

Hummus
on p.12

Buy it!

Per serving:

Calories 1,540 · **Total fat** 104.6g · **Sat. fat** 37g · **Protein** 47.9g

Carbohydrates 92.7g · **Sugar** 19.2g · **Sodium** 1,597mg · **Fiber** 27.6g

Sunday prep

Prepare the buckwheat and dressing in advance. Store in separate airtight containers in the fridge for around 2 days.

Buckwheat pho
with mackerel

Pho is a Vietnamese noodle soup with a clear broth, served with fresh herbs.

Ingredients

Serves 1

2 tbsp coconut oil

1 small fresh mackerel fillet, approx. 2½oz (75g), skin on or 2½oz (75g) canned mackerel, drained weight

1¾oz (50g) buckwheat noodles

1 green onion, finely chopped (reserve a few green bits to garnish)

1 tsp ginger root, finely chopped

1 garlic clove, crushed

1–2 tsp red chile, seeded and finely chopped

½ cup shiitake mushrooms, halved or sliced

½ cup broccoli, florets and stem, chopped

1 tsp miso paste (brown or white)

1 tsp tamari soy sauce

⅓ cup yellow bell pepper, julienned

1 tsp sesame seeds

1 sprig fresh basil

Method

1 Heat 1 tbsp of coconut oil in a frying pan over medium-high heat. Add the mackerel, skin-side down, and cook for 4 minutes. Turn and cook for 2 minutes, until cooked through. Remove and let cool.

2 Once cool, remove the skin, flake the fish into large chunks, and set aside. If using canned mackerel, drain and flake in the same way.

3 Cook the buckwheat noodles as per package instructions. Drain, rinse under cold water, and set aside.

4 Heat the remaining coconut oil in a pan over medium heat. Add the onion, ginger, garlic, and chile. Cook for 1–2 minutes, then add the mushrooms and broccoli and cook for 2 more minutes.

5 Dissolve the miso paste in 10fl oz (300ml) boiling water and add to the pan with the tamari. Bring to a boil, reduce the heat, and simmer for 5 minutes. Add the noodles, mackerel, and pepper to heat through.

6 Pour into a bowl and top with the sesame seeds, reserved green onion, and basil.

Boost it!
For an extra protein boost, top your bowl with half a soft-boiled egg.

Per serving:
Calories 648 · Total fat 38.8g · Sat. fat 22.3g · Protein 26.4g
Carbohydrates 47.9g · Sugar 6.2g · Sodium 399mg · Fiber 5.8g

Sunday prep

Prepare ingredients in advance. Put in a heatproof container (exclude coconut oil). Add 1¼ cups boiling water when you're ready to eat.

Pho *bowls*

This traditional Vietnamese soup can be adapted endlessly. All these variations retain the clear broth, the noodles, and the seasonings that give pho its distinctive, delicious flavor.

Chicken & Sriracha

Ingredients

1 small chicken fillet • 1 tbsp hoisin sauce • 1 tsp sesame seeds • Approx. 1¾oz (50g) dried brown rice noodles • 1 tbsp coconut oil • 1 green onion, chopped (plus garnish) • 1 tsp fresh ginger, finely chopped • 1 garlic clove, crushed • 1–2 tsp red chile, seeded, finely chopped • 4–5 green beans, julienned • 1 tsp miso paste • 1 tsp tamari soy sauce • ¼ cup bean sprouts • 1 tbsp fresh basil • 1 tbsp cashews, toasted and crushed • 1 radish, sliced • Sriracha sauce to taste • 1 lime wedge

Method

1 Preheat oven to 400°F (200°C). Rub the chicken with hoisin sauce, sprinkle with sesame seeds, and bake for 10–15 minutes until cooked through. Cool and shred the meat.
2 Cook the noodles as per package instructions. Drain, rinse in cold water, and set aside.
3 Heat the oil in a pan over medium heat. Add the onion, ginger, garlic, and chile. Cook for 1–2 minutes. Add the beans and cook for 2 minutes.
4 Dissolve miso in 1¼ cups boiling water and add to the pan with the tamari. Bring to a boil, reduce heat, and simmer for 5 minutes. Add 1⅓ cup chicken, the noodles, bean sprouts, and basil, then heat through for 1–2 minutes.
5 Put into a bowl; top with cashews, radish, and green onion. Drizzle on Sriracha; serve with lime.

Per serving:
Calories 650 • **Total fat** 26.6g • **Sat. fat** 12.4g
Protein 39.9g • **Carbohydrates** 62.5g
Sugar 10.9g • **Sodium** 1,031mg • **Fiber** 4.1g

Kelp & tofu

Ingredients

Approx. ¾oz (20g) dried kelp noodles (or seaweed spaghetti) · 1 tbsp coconut oil · 1 green onion, chopped (plus garnish) · 1 tsp fresh ginger, finely chopped · 1 garlic clove, crushed · 1–2 tsp red chile, seeded and finely chopped · 1 small carrot, julienned · 1 small bok choi · 1 stick lemongrass, halved, lightly bashed · 1 tsp miso paste · 1 tsp tamari soy sauce · 1¾oz (50g) firm, plain tofu, cubed · 1 tbsp macadamia nuts, toasted, crushed · 1 sprig of mint

Method

1 Cook the noodles as per package instructions. Drain, rinse in cold water, and set aside.
2 Heat the oil in a pan over medium heat. Add the onion, ginger, garlic, and chile. Cook for 1–2 minutes. Add the carrots, bok choi, and lemongrass and cook for 2 more minutes.
3 Dissolve the miso paste in 1¼ cups boiling water and add to the pan with the tamari soy sauce. Bring to a boil, reduce the heat, and simmer for 5 minutes. Add the noodles and tofu and heat through for 1–2 minutes.
4 Remove the lemongrass and discard.
5 Pour into a large serving bowl and top with macadamia nuts, the remaining green onion, and the mint.

Per serving:
Calories 389 · **Total fat** 33.3g · **Sat. fat** 12.6g
Protein 10.2g · **Carbohydrates** 11.8g
Sugar 7.5g · **Sodium** 543mg · **Fiber** 5g

Egg & shrimp

Ingredients

Approx. 1¾oz (50g) egg noodles · 1 tbsp coconut oil · 1 green onion, finely chopped (plus garnish) · 1 tsp fresh ginger, finely chopped · 1 garlic clove, crushed · 1–2 tsp red chile, seeded and finely chopped · ¼ cup kale, destalked and chopped · 1 tbsp dried dulce seaweed · 1 tsp miso paste · 1 tsp tamari soy sauce · 3–5 jumbo shrimp, ready to eat · 1 tbsp fresh cilantro, chopped (plus garnish) · ¼ small mango, diced · 1 tbsp peanuts, toasted and crushed · 1 lemon wedge

Method

1 Cook the noodles as per package instructions. Drain, rinse in cold water, and set aside.
2 Heat the oil in a pan over medium heat. Add the green onion, ginger, garlic, and chile. Cook for 1–2 minutes. Add the kale and dulce seaweed and cook for 2 more minutes.
3 Dissolve the miso paste in 1¼ cups boiling water and add to the pan with the tamari soy sauce. Bring to a boil, reduce the heat, and simmer for 5 minutes. Add the noodles, shrimp, and cilantro and heat through for 1–2 minutes.
4 Pour into a large serving bowl and top with the mango, peanuts, the remaining green onion, and a sprig of cilantro. Serve with the lemon wedge on the side.

Per serving:
Calories 505 · **Total fat** 22.7g · **Sat. fat** 12g
Protein 22.7g · **Carbohydrates** 56.1g
Sugar 17g · **Sodium** 812mg · **Fiber** 6.9g

Spicy harissa chicken & rice bowl

Chicken is full of protein, which your body needs for growth and repair.

Ingredients

Serves 1

1 chicken breast or thigh, cut into chunks

2 tbsp harissa marinade (see p.15)

¼ cup brown basmati rice

1 pinch of salt

1 tbsp olive oil

½ red bell pepper, sliced

½ zucchini, sliced

¼ cup kale, destalked and chopped

1–2 tbsp salsa verde (see p.15)

1 tbsp sliced almonds, lightly toasted

Salt and pepper to taste

Method

1 Preheat the oven to 400°F (200°C).

2 Place the chicken in a bowl with the harissa and let marinate while you prepare the rice and chop the vegetables.

3 Rinse the rice and place in a pan on the stove. Cover with water and bring to a boil with a pinch of salt. Turn down the heat and simmer for 30 minutes until the rice is soft.

4 Spread the chicken chunks on a baking pan and place in the oven for 10–15 minutes until cooked through.

5 Heat the olive oil in a griddle pan over medium-high heat. Add the pepper, zucchini, and kale to the pan and cook until the vegetables are softening—around 5 minutes.

6 Drain the rice and place in a serving bowl with the spicy chicken chunks and cooked vegetables. Serve with a heap of salsa verde and sprinkle with toasted almond flakes. Season with salt and pepper.

Make it!

Salsa verde
on p.15

Buy it!

Per serving:
Calories 733 · **Total fat** 35.8g · **Sat. fat** 5.2g · **Protein** 50.5g
Carbohydrates 58g · **Sugar** 12.8g · **Sodium** 429mg · **Fiber** 6.9g

Make it!

Harissa
on p.15

Buy it!

Zucchini noodles & roasted chickpeas

Chickpeas are a great source of zinc, which supports your immune system.

Ingredients

Serves 1

1 large carrot, coarsely chopped

1 tbsp olive oil

1 garlic clove, crushed

¼ tsp ground cumin

Cayenne pepper, a generous pinch

¼ tsp ground turmeric

Salt and pepper

½ cup chickpeas, ready to eat

½ cup kale, destalked and chopped

½ of a medium zucchini, spiralized

1–2 tbsp avocado pesto, plus extra to top (see p.15)

2½oz (75g) fresh mozzarella, sliced

1–2 tsp balsamic glaze, to taste (see p.15)

1 tbsp pine nuts, toasted

Method

1 Preheat the oven to 400°F (200°C). Spread the carrot on a baking sheet and toss with ½ tbsp olive oil, the garlic, cumin, cayenne, and turmeric. Season with salt and pepper. Roast in the oven for 10 minutes.

2 Remove from the oven and toss with the chickpeas, making sure everything is coated in spice. Return to the oven and roast for another 10 minutes.

3 In a small bowl, toss the kale with the remaining oil and a pinch of salt. Scrunch it together with your hands. Remove the baking sheet from the oven and add the kale. Roast for another 5 minutes.

4 Place the spiralized zucchini in a mixing bowl and cover with boiling water. Blanch for 1 minute, drain, and return to the bowl. Add the pesto and toss with the zucchini, then transfer to a serving bowl.

5 Top with the roasted chickpeas, vegetables, mozzarella, and more pesto. Drizzle with balsamic glaze, sprinkle with pine nuts, and season with salt and pepper.

Make it!

Avocado pesto & balsamic glaze
on p.15

Buy it!

Per serving:

Calories 801 · **Total fat** 62.6g · **Sat. fat** 15.5g · **Protein** 30.6g
Carbohydrates 31.9g · **Sugar** 14.3g · **Sodium** 563mg · **Fiber** 13.2g

Sunday prep

You can make the pesto and the glaze (see p.15) ahead. The pesto keeps for 1–2 days in the fridge, and the glaze for up to 6 months.

Spiced millet & vegetable bowl

Millet is rich in minerals and B vitamins to keep you feeling energized.

Ingredients

Serves 1

¼ cup millet flakes
½ cup butternut squash, cubed
½ cup broccolini
⅓ cup red bell pepper, sliced
½ tbsp coconut oil
½ tsp each mustard and cumin seeds
¼ onion, sliced
1 clove garlic, crushed
½ tsp green chile, finely chopped
1 tsp ginger, peeled and sliced
½ tsp curry powder
¾ cup vegetable stock
Salt and pepper to taste
3 tbsp cashews
3 tbsp plain yogurt
½ tbsp lime juice
2 tsp cilantro, chopped
1 wedge of lime

Method

1 Place the millet flakes in a frying pan. Dry toast them over high heat for 3–5 minutes until golden. Remove and set aside.

2 Put the squash and broccolini in a steaming pan (try to keep them separate) and steam for 4 minutes until softening. Add the red bell pepper and continue to steam for 1 minute.

3 Heat the oil in another pan over high heat. Add the mustard and cumin seeds and cook until they start to "pop." Reduce the heat and add the onion, garlic, chile, and ginger. Cook for 2–3 minutes, stirring until the onion softens. Add the curry powder and cook for 2 more minutes.

4 Add the millet flakes and stock to the spicy mixture and cook until the liquid absorbs. Season with a pinch of salt and set aside.

5 Toast the cashews in a frying pan over high heat for 3–4 minutes.

6 Prepare the dressing by combining the yogurt and lime juice.

7 Arrange the millet, squash, broccolini, and red bell pepper in a bowl. Add the nuts and a dollop of dressing. Garnish with cilantro and a wedge of lime. Season with salt and pepper to taste.

Per serving:
Calories 569 · **Total fat** 25.2g · **Sat. fat** 9.7g · **Protein** 21.5g
Carbohydrates 67.2g · **Sugar** 19.9g · **Sodium** 1,019mg · **Fiber** 8.1g

Broiled salmon teff & vegetable ribbons

Gluten-free supergrain teff is a great source of protein, iron, and calcium.

Ingredients

Serves 1

½ red bell pepper, cut lengthwise, stalk removed

½ zucchini, cut into thin strips

⅓ cup olive oil

2 large garlic cloves, peeled and halved

Salt and pepper to taste

¼ cup teff (brown or white)

¾ cup vegetable stock

1 small salmon fillet (skin on or off)

1 tsp capers

1 tbsp chives, chopped

1 sprig dill

1 lemon wedge

Method

1 Preheat the broiler to high. Broil the red pepper skin-side up for around 8 minutes until the skin starts to blister and char. Add the zucchini strips and heat for 2 minutes until soft. Remove the vegetables and set aside.

2 Pour the olive oil into a large jar and add the garlic. When cool enough to handle, peel the skin from the red pepper and slice into thin strips. Discard the skin.

3 Add the pepper and zucchini strips to the jar. Season with salt and pepper. Cover and marinate in the fridge for at least 1 hour.

4 Place the teff in a saucepan on the stove with the stock and simmer for 15 minutes, covered, until all the liquid has been absorbed.

5 Broil the salmon fillet under medium heat for 10–15 minutes, turning halfway through. Remove and allow to cool. Peel off the skin if necessary.

6 Once the teff has cooked, fluff up with a fork and place in a bowl. Top with the salmon fillet and the marinated vegetables. Garnish with capers, herbs, and the lemon wedge. Season with salt and pepper.

Per serving:
Calories 1,319 · **Total fat** 113.6g · **Sat. fat** 16.3g · **Protein** 30.1g
Carbohydrates 46.5g · **Sugar** 5.9g · **Sodium** 1,231mg · **Fiber** 6.5g

Spicy black bean
burrito bowl

This Mexican dish is full of fiber and protein to keep you feeling full.

Ingredients

Serves 1

¼ cup brown basmati rice

½ tbsp coconut oil

¼ onion, finely sliced

1 garlic clove, crushed

1 tsp red chile, finely chopped

½ cup black beans, ready
to eat

1 tbsp cilantro, chopped, plus extra
to garnish

6 cherry tomatoes, halved

3–4 tbsp guacamole (see p.15)

2 tbsp sour cream

1 lime wedge

Method

1 Place the rice in a saucepan on the stove, cover with water, and bring to a boil. Lower the heat and simmer, covered, for around 30 minutes until soft.

2 Heat the oil in a frying pan on the stove and add the onion and garlic. Cook for around 5 minutes until they start to soften.

3 Add the chile and cook for another 2 minutes.

4 Add the beans and cilantro, then cook for another 2 minutes until the beans are warmed through.

5 Drain the rice and place in a bowl.

6 Top with the tomatoes, guacamole, and spicy beans.

7 Garnish with a dollop of sour cream, the cilantro, and a wedge of lime.

Per serving:
Calories 549 · **Total fat** 27.9g · **Sat. fat** 15.3g · **Protein** 12.7g
Carbohydrates 65g · **Sugar** 10g · **Sodium** 338mg · **Fiber** 9g

Make it!

Guacamole
on p.15

Buy it!

Index

Acknowledgments

Kate Turner has been creating deliciously healthy, happy food for herself and her family for years. She loves good, honest, tasty meals that make you feel amazing, are packed full of natural energy, and are quick and easy to prepare.

Kate has a degree in health sciences, writes for magazines, and shares ideas on food, gardening, and family life on her blog homegrownkate.com. Other books include *Energy Bites* and *Superfood Breakfasts*, also for DK. Thanks and love go to Stanley, Scarlet, and Tommy for tasting, her mother for cleaning up, and her partner Will for everything else.

DK would like to thank: Louisa Carter, Charlotte Simpkins, and Ann Reynolds for recipe testing; Martha Burley for editorial assistance; and Hilary Bird for the index.